the night they met

the night they met

rob grose

the night they met

ISBN   978-1-7355764-2-8

Also by Rob Grose

A Word for the Word

This book is dedicated to my amazing wife, Lisa.

You are my precious partner in life and ministry.
Thank you for your unconditional love,
abiding faith, wise counsel, and
relentless pursuit of truth.

Many years later, looking back on the events of that night, he realized that the most significant moments in a lifetime rarely announce themselves in advance. Sure, someone might know that a big promotion, or graduation, or battle is looming before the next sunrise, but who really reflects with eternal gratitude about such intersections. No, the things of the heart, the providential appointments that change lives, come out of left field with a suddenness that defies pre-planning. At the point they are upon you, you are immediately just reacting; feeling and saying things that come from deeper inside of you than ever before. When later you replay them in your mind, you are forced to consider that perhaps you were swept along in an eternal plan for which you were created.

Prior to that moment it had been a day that had lived up to, or perhaps down to, his expectations for the first nineteen of the available 24 hours. He and a few hundred future Naval officers were spending two weeks in the southeastern tip of Virginia learning that you do not want to mess with the United States Marine Corps. That was particularly true of the Marine Gunnery Sergeant that currently commanded (and demanded) most minutes of his day. The first week with the Marines had been both physically and mentally demanding, but he admitted secretly to himself that it was sometimes fun. They had seen and done warrior exploits that he had never experienced before, and he felt that he had measured very favorably against his peers.

However, that night was different. Most of his fellow Midshipmen looked with excitement and energy to the night at the Little Creek Officers' Club, mixing with the opposite sex and away from the watchful eyes of the sergeants. Surprisingly, he had very little enthusiasm and energy for the evening's diversion. It would be two weeks later before his lagging energy would be diagnosed as a severe case of mononucleosis. The bottom line was that he was tired and he quickly realized that there were a lot more men than women crowding the Officers' Club that night. He had a plan: Just enough time for one tour around the club and he would be on the bus back to the barracks for a long night of much needed sleep. Yes, that plan would be both prudent and profitable considering the additional training that awaited him the next day.

At that moment, his night and his life, would be changed forever. He saw her at a distance through a doorway arch and the sight stopped him in his tracks. The guy walking behind him ran into his back with a thud and a light splash of whatever he was drinking. He did not even care that his neatly pressed white uniform had been accidentally misted. Every bit of his being told him to stop and hold whatever position was required to keep that view. She was smiling in his direction and he immediately (and illogically) claimed that smile as intended for him.

It was a smile that he had to see again. To his fellow midshipmen it was a challenging look that said "try your best, most clever lines on me; but I'll still prove to be more resourceful than you". One look into her bright, radiant eyes and he concluded that she <u>really was</u> more clever than any of these future aviators, submariners, marines, and ship-drivers who were competing for her attention. From thirty feet away and less than ten seconds flat he concluded without a doubt that she was both bright <u>and</u> incredibly beautiful. Decades of first-hand experience would offer no evidence to refute the accuracy of his assessment in those first ten seconds.

He faced an immediate set of significant obstacles. This beautiful young woman was surrounded by a dozen of his fellow midshipmen, each waiting for their chance to say or do something meaningful in her presence. The moment demanded a strategy and tactics beyond any he had employed before (and would ever again!) His listlessness of a moment earlier was instantly replaced by the adrenaline of anticipation and apprehension. Anticipation, because he promised himself that he would not leave the building without meeting this exquisite creature; and apprehension, because he had no idea what he would say or do given that opportunity.

The first challenge was to observe her without appearing to stalk her. Fortunately, he knew almost every man in the club and he would not face a situation where he would have to stand alone, leaning against a wall in obvious, gawking silence. Unfortunately, the club had many rooms and he was forced to pursue her room-to-room which made it difficult to remain undetected.

"So, you tailing the brunette?" was the question/accusation minutes later from an observant classmate. Yes, and he was not the only one. As he answered the question in the affirmative, he realized that he was so focused on her eyes and her smile that he had failed to note some of the other obvious and readily available facts. Her hair was beautiful, long and brown. *When she smiled, her eyes lit up the room and ignited something deep in his heart.* Her thin, graceful arms revealed the tan of a woman who was enjoying the summer on the local beaches. *When she smiled, her eyes lit up the room and ignited something deep in his heart.* Her floor-length conservative dress (red on the top and white on the bottom...his school colors!) could not totally conceal her athletic figure. *When she smiled, her eyes lit up the room and ignited something deep in his heart.* Her makeup and jewelry were tasteful, not overdone. *When she smiled, her eyes lit up the room and ignited something deep in his heart.* She moved from conversation to conversation with what appeared to him as confidence, grace, and purpose. And *when she smiled, her eyes lit up the room and ignited something deep in his heart.*

This woman would not be impressed with "pickup lines" or "war stories". She had probably heard them all in that one night. He needed to know more about her! As that thought filled his mind, he noticed the repeating transition take place as one midshipman said goodbye and another approached to ask her name. More than a dozen men had spoken or danced with her and he had not even gotten within twenty feet. Wait a minute...that was his answer! Those guys possessed some of the information about her that he wanted so desperately to know.

For the next forty minutes he tracked down every guy he knew that had spoken with her. Slowly he pieced together all that he could learn about this woman of his obsession. Her name was Lisa. She was the daughter of a Captain, a Naval Aviator, who currently commanded an air wing based in Norfolk. Her parents were moving soon to a new duty station in Iceland, but she would be returning for her sophomore year at Mary Baldwin College in the mountains of western Virginia.

He had gathered some invaluable information, but how would he put it to use? While contemplating that question an unexpected opportunity presented itself. The current pursuer had momentarily abandoned her near the dance floor to (presumably) acquire beverages. The opening was brief, but clearly available. Surprising himself, he strode to a point directly in front of her. Standing as straight and confidently as possible, he boldly introduced himself and asked her name. Before she could reply, he answered his own question. She smiled, but did not seem particularly impressed or amused (any number of people in the building probably knew her name). Undeterred, he asked another question and then quickly answered it himself using more of her personal information he had learned earlier. With each subsequent question and answer she seemed more amused by, and curious about, the industrious young man standing before her.

As he neared the inevitable end of this one-sided question and answer introduction, he caught a glimpse of the previous pursuer returning with a drink in each hand. The dance floor offered an immediate refuge from the impending interruption. He prayed that he had earned a dance.

Apparently he had, because she took his right hand when it was offered and followed him to another spot on the wooden floor. He would never forget that initial touch of their hands. Two thoughts immediately flooded his brain. First, her hand fit perfectly in his. Not just conveniently close to fitting comfortably together, but more like they were perfectly cast for each other. Second, the nerve endings in his fingertips had never been so sensitive. Not only could he feel her fingers against his, but it seemed like the smallest ridges in their fingerprints were deeply interlocking. He would never tire of holding that hand.

To the casual observer their first dance was respectful and appropriate to the setting. To him, it was amazingly intimate. The intimacy came not from the physical contact, but from the accompanying verbal and non-verbal conversation. It was a comfortable, familiar conversation. They spoke almost as if they had met before and sensed the assurance of a lifetime left to share. The words flowed from his heart as he spoke about his life to that point and learned more about hers. Her words revealed the character and intelligence he had sensed from across the room. She was smart, but not aloof. She was playful, but not flirtatious. She listened well, answered with confidence, asked probing questions, and never broke eye contact. For that he was grateful. Lost in her eyes and her touch and her voice, he became temporarily oblivious to the other people and conversations swirling around them.

Their obvious rapt attention to each other must have discouraged her other suitors because they were able to dance and talk and move throughout the club and adjoining outside balcony without interruption for the next hour. Inside of him during that fantastic fleeting hour, there was an ironic battle going on. His brain kept thinking that conversation and human contact had never been so pure and effortless. Meanwhile, despite the adrenaline, his body felt a fatigue that he had never experienced in his first twenty years. He began to worry that, in his exhaustion and growing lightheadedness, he might say something to ruin a conversation that was more precious to him than any he had ever had.

How could he part from this amazing woman? How would she interpret the first signs of tiredness that might signal a lack of serious interest? And he <u>was</u> SERIOUSLY INTERESTED! He felt a kind of anticipatory joy and desire that was completely new and exhilarating.

All of the conflicting energy and emotions within him precipitated his first real tactical error of the evening. Without warning or even a moment of preparatory silence, he thanked her for a wonderful time, announced that he was "about to drop in his boots" (where did those words come from?) and would need to call it a night. He turned and, as gracefully as possible, headed to the club door, expecting the shuttle bus to be waiting immediately outside. To his dismay, the shuttle had just departed.

With no place to wait outside, he returned inside seeking a spot to sit and rest until the bus returned. The chairs near the door were occupied, so he slowly moved back across the club looking for something to sit or lean upon. He found an open spot of wall and he turned to find his eyes meeting hers again. This look was not as enchanting as their first.

Across the room, her verbal conversation was with someone else, but her non-verbal expressions were speaking directly to him. "I thought you were exhausted and leaving for the night" was the first sarcastic volley he caught from her posture. "I don't understand why you are still here if you were too tired to stay with me" came from the questioning angle of her lips pressed together. Finally, her eyes said "I wish we had more time to get to know each other". He clung tightly to that last message as he leaned there pondering how and why he could so clearly read the thoughts of someone he had just met that night.

About the time that he resolved to approach her and try to explain his reappearance, a commotion near the door indicated that the shuttle bus had just returned. He made his way toward the door and onto the bus, intentionally choosing a seat away from the rest of the midshipmen. At that moment he did not feel like sharing a seat...or his thoughts about that night. His assessment of the evening was bringing on a strange mixture of elation and frustration. He had met an amazing, beautiful young woman. Against all odds, he had won the opportunity to keep her company and her attention for much of the evening. In his haste, he had walked away from her presence without her phone number, her address, or even the slightest indication that they would ever meet again!

Arriving at the barracks, he waved his ID at the midshipman on duty and slowly climbed the stairs to the floor where his company and platoon were berthed. He tore off his white uniform and fell into his bunk. Despite his mononucleosis-induced exhaustion, the sleep he dearly needed did not come easily.

Questions flooded his brain. How could he have left without her phone number? If he was able to contact her, would she agree to meet again before he left for Texas in a little over a week? Would her family see him as just another midshipman impressed by an officer's daughter? Did he imagine the intimacy between them? Was she thinking of him at that moment?

Suddenly, he felt a wave of certainty and peace. The amazing connection they had experienced that night was not something he had imagined. He resolved that whatever it took he would not leave town without seeing her again.

As he drifted off to sleep, his heart and his mind came to a startling, but unanimous, conclusion: That night he had met the woman created for a lifelong union with him. For the first time in his life, he fell asleep focused on the thoughts and desires of another human being.

Rob Grose, a graduate of Cornell University and Dallas Theological Seminary, was a Naval Aviator and a businessman in the IT consulting industry prior to his calling to pastoral ministry. He lives in Richmond, Virginia with his amazing wife, Lisa.